THE MONASTIC LIFE

A Most Beneficial Dialogue Between An
Orthodox Monk and A Contemporary
Theologian

by

METROPOLITAN CYPRIAN
OF OROPOS AND FILI

Translated From the Greek

by

Bishop Chrysostomos of Oreoi
and Hieromonk Auxentios

CENTER FOR TRADITIONALIST ORTHODOX
STUDIES

Etna, California 96027

Augustinian Novitiate
Racine, WI 53402

Translated from the Greek text

(Athens, 1970)

Library of Congress Catalog Card Number

© 1988 by
CENTER FOR TRADITIONALIST
ORTHODOX STUDIES
All rights reserved

ISBN 0-911165-11-8

About the Author

His Eminence, the Most Rev. Cyprian, Lic. Theol., Dr. Theol. (*honoris causa*), is Metropolitan of Oropos and Fili and President of the Synod of Bishops of the True (Old Calendar) Orthodox Church of Greece. A former clergyman of the State Church of Greece, he returned several decades ago to the Old Calendar along with the monastery which he serves as Bishop-Abbot, the Holy Monastery of Sts. Cyprian and Justina in Fili, just outside Athens, Greece. His Eminence and the monastery brotherhood embraced the traditionalist Orthodox movement in the face of fears that ecumenical excesses and innovation in the Faith were compromising the age-old witness of the Orthodox Church of Greece. Despite this move and the severe persecution that they suffered in following the dictates of their consciences, the monastery brotherhood and the Metropolitan have remained resolute in their moderate and circumspect attitude towards contemporary trends in the Church of Greece, working sedulously for the return of the Greek Mother Church to the fullness of Orthodox Tradition.

Spiritual son of the renowned Elder, Archimandrite Philotheos Zervakos, Metropolitan Cyprian was tonsured to the Small Schema at the famous Monastery of St. John on the island of Patmos. He is known in Greece as a confessor and spiritual guide, and the large and flourishing monastery which he heads is known throughout the Orthodox world for its spiritual aid to those suffering from the effects of psychic charlatanism and demonic possession. His Eminence's some twenty books and many writings have been translated into English and French, among other languages, and his missionary work reaches out from his Greek homeland to America, Sweden, Italy, and Africa. An eloquent lecturer, Metropolitan Cyprian maintains a demanding schedule, dividing his time between instruction, Church administration, and the spiritual life. He resides in his monastery in Fili.

Dedication

(from the original Greek text)

The present work is dedicated to my spiritual children, indissolubly bound to me through love in Christ, with the hope that we shall never be separated, either in this age or in the age to come.

The Author

Contents

Introduction by Bishop Chrysostomos	7
Prologue	15
Chapter 1	17
Chapter 2	23
Chapter 3	28
Chapter 4	34
Chapter 5	38
Chapter 6	40
Chapter 7	44
Epilogue	46
Notes	48

6   The Monastic Life

Metropolitan Cyprian

INTRODUCTION

Some years ago, while reading through a number of his inspiring spiritual and theological books and tracts, I happened upon a book on monasticism by Metropolitan Cyprian of Oropos and Fili, my spiritual Father. Having begun to translate some of his works into English, I was looking for other appropriate texts. I quickly scanned this book, thinking, because of many of the profound Patristic quotations contained in it, that it must be a deep theological treatise more appropriate for a Patristic scholar than an ordinary monk or Orthodox layman. As I examined the book more closely, however, I was struck by the relevance of much of what I was reading for the general reader —indeed, for the Orthodox monk and layman as well as the sincere non-Orthodox Christian with an interest in the Christian East. After a careful and complete reading, I decided that the book, which beautifully and convincingly addresses itself to many of the misconceptions that modern Christians, Orthodox and heterodox alike, have about monasticism, had to be translated.

My responsibilities as an Abbot and college professor, two duties which for some time I fulfilled simultaneously, and more lately as a Bishop, prevented me from realizing my intention of translating His Eminence's small volume on the monastic life. Now, however, I have found the time to undertake this pleasant task, partly because of the efforts of Metropolitan Cyprian himself. During a trip to Sweden two years ago, His Eminence met with several faculty members of the renowned Theological Institute of Uppsala University, the country's oldest and most prestigious institution of higher learning. The outcome of those talks was my appointment to the Theological Institute as a Visiting Associate Professor in Patristics and the Psychology of Religion. It is in this capacity, and as part of my research at Uppsala, that I am preparing this translation.

I must, therefore, thank Metropolitan Cyprian, firstly, for allowing me to translate his excellent book and for arranging my visit to Sweden; and, secondly, I must express my gratitude to the faculty of the Theological Institute of Uppsala University for their great kindness to me and for their contributions to my research and writing. I must also thank the many fine and enthusiastic students, not only at the university, but at the Johannelund Theological Institute —where I have lodged while in Sweden—, who have made my appointment at Uppsala such a pleasant experience. Were it not for these contributions and for this pleasantness, I might not have so easily finished this small volume.

Assisting me in my work here in Sweden has been the Steward of the St. Gregory Palamas Monastery—where I reside in the U.S.—, Hieromonk Auxentios. Father Auxentios is a doctoral student at the Graduate Theological Union, Berkeley, and has spent a semester working at Uppsala as part of an independent studies program. He has, during this time, unselfishly and diligently applied his translating skills in helping me to render the Metropolitan's wise words about monasticism into an English style that adequately captures the lyric beauty of parts of the Greek text. I am much indebted to Father Auxentios for his work.

Metropolitan Cyprian's book on monasticism is entitled, *A Most Beneficial Dialogue Between an Orthodox Monk and a Contemporary Theologian.* While this title is not unusual for books written in the far more expressive style of the Greek language, it seemed wise to me to provide a shorter title for the English version of the book; hence, the present title. However, I have, for the sake of allegiance to the original, retained the Greek title of the book as a subtitle. I have also somewhat revised the original Greek text by omitting a few expressions which, when translated into English, lose some of the relevance that they hold for the Metropolitan's Greek commentary. In Greek, unlike English, style itself often conveys subtle meanings that are simply lost in translation. I have felt it best not to belabor points by supplementing such difficult-to-translate expressions with long philological commentaries. Despite all of this, I believe that the text herein presented is loyal to His Eminence's original essay and that no essential arguments or elements have been lost in my editorial adjustments.

In the modern age, we are almost ignorant of history. The triumph of technology has brought with it a kind of intellectual amnesia, such that we think that all things are the products of the world around us. Technological change during this century has been so striking and so fast, that we attribute almost everything to the present and nothing to the past. We do not look to the past as our forefathers did. We are victims of an exaggerated appreciation for the present. So it is that monasticism is so misunderstood today. Modern man knows little of the history of this institution, nor is he aware of the contributions that it has made to civilization.

In Eastern Christianity, the greatest Fathers and

theologians of the Church have come from the monastic ranks of the Church. Indeed, during the Arian captivity of the Church and throughout the fierce conflicts of the Iconoclastic Controversy, it was often the monastics who consistently held up the standard of the Faith, over and against the higher Church authorities, many of whom succumbed to heresy and error. It is not strange, therefore, that in the Orthodox Church we often measure the health of a local Church by the number and quality of its monastic institutions. Monasticism has traditionally served as a barometer for monitoring the spiritual life. A Church with rich monastic roots is always a healthier Church —so theory and historical data teach the Eastern Christian.

In the West, where the demise of the Latin center of the Roman Empire in the early centuries of Christianity led to a complete breakdown in political and social life, Christianity filled this void. Its hierarchy began to fill the political vacuum by the integration of secular power into the ecclesiastical hierarchy (though this initially positive move eventually led to a Papal monarchy and the departure of Western Christianity from the world of Orthodox Christianity). And in the social realm, the Church's monastics undertook to care for the needs of the people. The first hospitals, the first schools and universities, and the first great libraries of the modern era began with the efforts of monastics. Monastic communities fostered the growth of towns and preserved, in the remnants of an Empire ravaged by barbarian conquests, the rudiments of civilization.

If we have forgotten these things about monasticism in the modern age, we must also admit that Western monasticism has changed over the centuries. Certainly monastics do not today constitute the percentage of the population that they did in the Christian West in past centuries. Moreover, Western Christian monasticism has not only become something far more oriented toward social service than the mystical monastic life of the Christian East, but it has been almost totally transformed in America during the past two decades. Monks and nuns in street clothes, standing forth as advocates of social justice and political reform, are the standard American image of the monastic. Traditional habit-clad contemplatives have been relegated to the stale pages of history or have become the stuff of cartoon strips and buffoons to be exploited in television commercials.

Though Eastern Christian monastics, too, have declined in number, they nonetheless hold forth in far greater numbers than Western Christian monastics. That they dot the communist-dominated countries of Eastern Europe with noticeable frequency is probably good evidence of the health and fortitude of this Orthodox monastic life. Also, in general, Orthodox monasticism has remained, in keeping with the more profound philosophical foundations of the Eastern Christian witness, fundamentally focused on the task of human transformation. Union with God through the conquest of the passions and the cleansing of the mind and body is still the essential goal of the Eastern Christian monastic aspirant. *Theosis*, or divinization, a participation of man in the Divine Energies of God, is still the primary purpose of Christian life for the Orthodox monk or nun.

To some extent, this purer Orthodox monasticism has suffered in modern times, particularly, again, in America, where heterodox monastic communities have converted to the Orthodox Faith and have introduced into the Church's monastic life ideas and practices that are wholly foreign to her. However, these aberrations are neither numerous enough nor well enough known to account for the contemporary ignorance of genuine Orthodox monasticism that prevails in our times. This ignorance stems again from the lack of knowledge of the past that so marks our a-historical age.

Given all of this, nothing could be more timely than a book which portrays a confrontation between a traditional Orthodox monk and a contemporary Orthodox theologian. Not only can such a book restore to us a more realistic and accurate view of what monasticism is in its traditional form —in that form which still characterizes, as we have said, the vast majority of Eastern Orthodox monasticism—, but it can teach us much about the problems that face contemporary Orthodoxy. For, if the Western Christian can recapture, in a discourse on true Orthodox monasticism, the roots of Western monasticism itself, the Orthodox Christian can find in such an essay the roots of a Faith which, at least in Western Europe and America, is very quickly being distorted and transformed into that which it is not.

Metropolitan Cyprian pinpoints the Western captivity of the Orthodox Church by pitting the presumably pistareen beliefs of a traditional monastic against the rationalistic assumptions of a "contemporary" Orthodox theologian. The theologian in question will immediately strike anyone immersed in the spiritual traditions of the Orthodox East as an expositor *par excellence* of Western Christian concepts and of a certain spirit of modernism unknown to the genuine, unchanging wisdom of the Christian East. The Westerner will no doubt find the theologian's ideas familiar and apropos. This tells us something about the state of modern Orthodox theology, which has indeed deviated, in many circles, from Holy Tradition.

If this little volume, then, can restore us to an understanding of Orthodox monasticism as it has flourished for countless centuries in Orthodox lands, it can also lead us to break away from the Western captivity which led Russian theologians of the eighteenth century to embrace such Latinisms as the Immaculate Conception, and which has led to the perversion of Orthodox Patristics that is sometimes today known as "neo-Orthodoxy" among certain *avant-garde* Greek theologians. Within a true understanding of the angelic life, the monastic struggle for Christian perfection, we can find a corrective for the deviations to the right and to the left that have left the Orthodox world in our times divided between those who firmly hold to the Christian traditions passed down to us by the Apostles themselves, and the beliefs and doctrines that have been formed from an adherence to the caprice and fancy of successive ages, which in turn have debased the pristine truth of Christianity and have made it unrecognizable to the faithful and devout follower of Christ.

Monasticism is not something unto itself —a peculiar and exclusive institution. In the true monastic every Christian sees what he can be. He beholds a model to be emulated. He embraces the higher faculties of the soul and beholds what it is that embodies all that to which Christians aspire. As an old adage has it: "Christ, the light of Angels; Angels, the light of monastics; monastics, the light of the laity." Monasticism reaches up to Christ, derives from Christ, and brings the Christian Faithful into a direct encounter with the light that flows forth from Christ and His Angels.

Just as the body has need of various victuals and craves the things that sustain it, so the soul needs an image of purity. It is this image which the monk and nun have always presented. Monastics who have fallen short of this image have often scandalized and disappointed the souls of the Faithful. But the many more monastics who have upheld this image and who have lived in absolute purity and virginity have exalted the souls of Christians for centuries. It is such monastics that the present book portrays. Any who do not understand this, and who are burdened by the demonic temptation to forego a vision of the successful and true monastic for the frightful sight of the pseudo-monastics who have gained the attention of the irreligious modern man —soothed, as he is, by all which reinforces his misbelief—, will find no benefit in this book. Anyone, however, who wishes to glimpse the genuine Christian in his purest form will delight in this little book on the philosophical life which is monasticism.

Bishop Chrysostomos of Oreoi
Uppsala, Sweden
1987

PROLOGUE

> "How beautiful and good the practice of silence. Indeed, how beautiful and good. So sweet its yoke, so light its burden. A sweet existence, a practice of delight."
> *Evagrios the Monk*

The Holy Fathers of our Orthodox Faith, "being destitute, afflicted, tormented, of whom the world was not worthy, ...wandered in deserts, and in mountains, and in dens and caves of the earth," and offered themselves up as vessels of the Holy Spirit; they excelled as brilliant illuminators, "interpreted the Mysteries of Holy Scripture and established Canons, elucidated matters dogmatic," warred against heretics, and were thus shown forth as pillars and exemplars of holiness.

Through fasting, vigils, and prayers, living in monasteries or amidst the wild and inhospitable crags of the desert, "nestled" within these spiritual eagles' haunts, far from the world, conversing with the "friend of the desert," sweet Jesus, they succeeded, by His Grace, in being united to the Holy Trinity, in becoming gods.

Today, however, as we pass through a fearful age of confusion and apostasy, we see not only atheists, but Christian believers, too —whether out of ignorance or out of a willful desire not to see the truth—, rallying forth against this divinely-established institution of monasticism, wishing to see monastics removed far from their spiritual arena, the desert.

They wish to see them in the world, in order to "benefit" those living therein, and to see them cease being so-called "social parasites," "bums", and "useless entities."

In our efforts to enlighten, by the Providence of the Lord, those who have, in embracing such a view, failed to grasp the truth, we have recounted in this little book a conversation between a brother of our monastery (whose name herein is fictitious) and a young theologian on the subject in question.

Hoping that my brothers in Christ will be benefited by the reading of this book, I ask that they beseech the Lord that monasticism might once again shine forth in all of its glory and cease to be unjustly slandered and considered a supposedly outmoded institution which has no meaning whatever today for the sinful world.

Also, I would ask that the reader pray for me and for our Brotherhood in Christ.

At The Holy Monastery of Sts. Cyprian and Justina
in Fili, Attica,
September 26, 1970 (Old Style)
The Feast of St. John the Theologian

The Abbot,
Archimandrite Cyprian
(now Metropolitan of Oropos and Fili)

Chapter One

"He who has tasted of things above readily disdains those things below."

(St. John of the Ladder)

We had just finished daily Vespers at our monastery and Father Isaac, along with a young theologian, retreated to the Eastern end of the cells, where there was greater vegetation. A soft breeze rustled in the leaves of the trees, and the two of them sensed the mystical "Cries" of nature pervading the atmosphere. The fragrance of the flowers was wafting up "as incense before Thee." The buzzing of the insects and the chirping of the birds had joined the mystical music of nature and offered up praise to the Creator. Nature was chanting its Vespers. Darkness began to overshadow the landscape. The sun had just sunk behind the mountains, casting a golden hue over the horizon and wonderfully framing the singing things of nature.

Father Isaac and the theologian sat down under a pine tree and remained silent for some time. This made the young theologian uneasy and, unable to endure any longer, he broke the silence.

THEOLOGIAN: So this, Father, is the life of the monk? In the morning we attended the Divine Liturgy. In the late morning the Hours. In the afternoon the Ninth Hour and Vespers. And this evening we will attend Compline and Matins. Your work is little. The conversation between you is limited. A certain melancholy atmosphere reigns over the entire monastery. How can a person endure this? Everyday the same thing, the same monotony, the same oppressing things. ...What keeps you in this desolate place?

MONK: The monk, my child —Father Isaac answered—, is "by force of nature a continual and perfect guard over the senses." The monk attempts always to see within his heart and, by the Grace of God, to cleanse it of the passions. Therefore he never thinks about whether a place is desolate or beautiful. By turning inwardly, he cuts himself off from all external things. What he at all times tries to do is to converse only with the Bridegroom of his soul, Christ. Christ comforts him and He covers him with His Grace, so that the place in which he finds himself does not concern him. We read in the Fathers that Amma Sara, though she lived above a certain river for sixty-two years, never went down to see it —to wonder at it, as we would say today. When a monk is soothed by the wellsprings of Divine Love, he has no desire even to leave his cell. The monk lives continually in the Divine.

THEOLOGIAN: But this I cannot understand — the young theologian interrupted. If a monk cares only for himself and for his "little cell," separated from the world, uncommunicative, how does he put into practice the love which is an essential trait of a Christian? Is this not, therefore, just egotism?

MONK: Listen, my child. The greatest joy and delight of God is to dwell in the pure hearts of those who love Him. Since, therefore, the goal of the monastic, as with every Christian, is to be united to God by Grace, to be "divinized," all of his fervor is directed toward cleansing his heart of the passions and making it a bright throne and chamber where the Holy Trinity might dwell. For this reason, St. Gregory Palamas says, "Indeed, only this is impossible to God, to enter into union with man before he has been cleansed." Consequently, it is not egotism for a monk to attempt in solitude to deliver himself from the dung of the passions. Far more moved is God when you overcome the passions, than when you return thousands of souls to goodness, as the Fathers say.

THEOLOGIAN: Excuse me, Father —the young theologian interjected—, but it seems that by all of this you mutilate the teachings of the Gospel and distort it. For all that the Lord said about our concern for our neighbor, what you have told me could be written in the margins. Where are charity for the poor, aid, compassion? Where the, "Go ye and teach all nations..."? How will we raise the fallen sinner from the mire of sin if we do not draw near and extend a hand to him? If everyone is closed up in monasteries, what will become of those who have need of a sermon or a word of exhortation to abandon the way of the devil and to set upon the path toward God, toward salvation?

MONK: You have so many mistaken ideas about monks, my brother. God has assigned each one of the Faithful to a particular place where he might work out his salvation. Some live in the world. Correspondingly, they offer works of charity for their neighbors in the struggle for their souls. Some occupy themselves with preaching, others with philanthropy. Some work in hospitals and in convalescent centers, while, indeed, some live as monks in the desert. Each one struggles in the place to which he has been assigned. All of these pursuits are good and holy when performed for the glory of God. But it is not right that all should be assigned to the same task in life, that of philanthropy and social action. This is criminal and senseless. Every individual has a different vocation and different spiritual strengths. As St. Isaac the Syrian says: "The height of your calling, O Monk, is loftier than that of men who perform deeds of charity. Do not —I beg of you—, do not subject yourself to this way. For charitable works are like the food of children and appropriate for the worldly. But silence bound to the life of poverty reaches to the pinnacle of perfection."

Good works have always served merely to offer an example and are of secondary import. [1] Our Lord promises that those who shall "see" Him are the "pure in heart." And for this reason He specifically blesses *them*, not those who perform many acts of philanthropy. The heart, the "seat" of the soul, must be purified by the Grace of the Lord. To be sure, then and only then does the believer unerringly know the Divine Will "in every time and place and matter."

THEOLOGIAN: But Elder —the young theologian once again interrupted—, before that verse of the Beatitudes is one which says, "Blessed are the merciful, for they shall obtain mercy." [In the Greek, literally, "Blessed are the charitable, for they shall be shown charity."] Therefore, works of charity take precedence.

MONK: Yes, my friend, but we must fully understand what is meant by the word "charity" here. According to Patristic terminology, "charity" does not refer to the giving of something material to a person in order to meet some physical need, though it does encompass this meaning. More properly and correctly, one is "charitable" when he feels the pain of his brother, when he suffers with his brother in his afflictions and worries, when he feels compassion for his brother's sins, and when he continually prays for his brother —often more so than for himself! [2] This becomes obvious when we realize that not all men have the means to offer charity in the form of goods. Indeed, if one has a heart rich with the Grace of God, that is, a heart that is charitable according to the desire of God ("Be ye therefore merciful [charitable], as your Father also is merciful"), then he is of greater benefit to the suffering and needy through his prayer —for one must consider that those in whom God dwells are able even to change His Will by their prayers.

In this regard, the words of Abba Isaac the Syrian are especially poignant. Having so greatly impressed me, I committed them to memory: "What, then, is a merciful heart? A heart burning for the whole of creation, for men, for birds, for animals, for demons, and for every creature. Eyes running with tears at seeing and recalling all of these. From great and profound charity, pressing hard within it, and from its far-reaching forbearance, the heart is subdued and is unable to bear, to hear, or to behold the befalling of any harm or even slight sorrow upon creation. It is thus, too, that a man, out of the great charity that stirs without measure in his heart, according to the likeness of God, will offer up tearful prayers at every hour for the irrational beasts, for the enemies of truth, for those who might harm him, and even for reptiles —that they might be protected and shown mercy." [3] "The preciseness and perfection of charity are seen in the forbearance of those who prefer to suffer wrongs.... If you wish to attain to the virtue of charity, first accustom yourself to the scorn of all things temporal, so that your mind will not be attracted to them and thus go out beyond its own limits...."

Chapter Two

"Love is begotten by prayer."

THEOLOGIAN: You are telling me many new things, Elder, that they do not teach us at the university. But if what you tell me about material charity is really true, what can you tell me about preaching? If those who fear God go to monasteries and convents, who will preach the Word of God when the flock is hungry to hear?

MONK: So that I do not tire you with my words and so that you do not think that I am expressing my own opinions and offering "novel doctrines," I will quote in full an appropriate passage from St. Isaac the Syrian: "It is good for one to teach men the way of God and to take them from evil to the knowledge of Divine Providence, from error to divine knowledge, for this is the way of Christ and the Apostles, and there is, in such, much that is lofty and soul-saving. If, however, a man feels within himself that he ails in his spiritual perception of things, that his quest is being thwarted, or that his understanding has been obscured because his mind once again needs protection and his senses need to be brought into subjection, or because, in treating others, his own soul has lost its healthiness, by the freedom of his own will, and has succumbed to the agitation of his mind —let such a man recall the Apostolic *dictum*, which tells us that strong meat befits those who are perfect, and let him abstain from teaching others, that he not hear again, 'Physician, heal thyself!' Let him judge himself and let him restore the health of his soul, and instead of his audible words of instruction, let him teach other men through his virtuous way of life and his good works.... I believe that thus, being far from men, he can better benefit them, in his zeal for good works [4], than he can by being a neighbor who teaches through words, when he himself might be sick in soul and in need of a physician. For when a blind man leads a blind man, both deserve to fall into a hole...."

THEOLOGIAN: Indeed, these things seem quite correct, Elder. But I cannot understand the following. On account of the passions, all men are ailing. Who, then, is left for philanthropy, preaching, and so on, in so far as one must be perfect to undertake these things?

MONK: Ah, my child, do not misinterpret Patristic and Scriptural passages and teachings. In those things which I have related to you, I have wished to protect you from the danger of thinking that works, above all, are the aim of the Christian life and that monks, consequently, since they do not do works, are not sociable, do not have love, and are social parasites. Works are performed, but with corresponding exercises in humility and with a full knowledge that works alone do not save a man. [5] In its failure to understand this, the Papacy, for example, has become a world-wide philanthropic foundation which lacks, however, the Holy Spirit. If works were able to save us, if, as the Latins claim, they over-abound so as to save others, then in vain did the Lord come upon the earth, become man, and suffer crucifixion for us. For there were before Christ people who were far more charitable than we.

THEOLOGIAN: From what you say, Father, I see that a man's salvation is independent of other men. That is to say, on the Day of Judgment God will not say, for example, to the monk or the hermit, and so on that to enter the abodes of Heaven, "You must show me what you did for your neighbor." Is that right?

MONK: No, my son, you have misunderstood. When a monk is sanctified in the desert life and made to be a dwelling place for God, his heart is so much filled with love..., well, to understand, let us once again turn to Abba Isaac: "Paradise is the love of God, within which are the delights of all of the Beatitudes." Gehenna is the deprivation of the love of God, and those "who are punished in Gehenna are scourged with the whip of love." Yet in another place, this great Saint tells us that "he who has reached perfection" loves, because of God and in God, "all equally and without discrimination." Also, remember Abba Agathon, the desert Father, who said, "I wished to find a leper and take his body, giving him my own." Thus, the good works performed by many are not even evidence of true love. We do not acquire love *through* philanthropic works (in which pride, vainglory, and conceit are too often hidden); rather, true love disposes us *towards these things*. He who has love has God. But to have God, you must have waged a personal warfare against your passions, against the monster which is called "I," against egotism. "Love," St. Isaac tells us, "is the fruit of prayer." "Love of God is found in the denial of one's self." Who among those who boast of their good works has genuine love? Who would give his healthy body to a leper and take the leper's as his own? Abba Agathon was able to say what he did because he had first loved God by surrendering himself into God's hands within the desert, where, through ascetic struggle and humility, he cleansed his soul and was made an abode of the Holy Trinity. And since he lived in God, he loved as God loves, for "God is love." So God, on the Day of Judgment, *will* demand love and evidence of love towards one's neighbor.

THEOLOGIAN: There, Elder, now you are agreeing with me! So, what will the monk present to God?

MONK: Please, my son, attend to what I say, so that I need not repeat myself. The monk's demonstration of love toward his neighbor is the prayer that he offers for his neighbor. If you wish me to be more explicit, pure and unadulterated love is encountered at the time of prayer, when the believer, hidden in the treasury of his heart —far away from all display and vainglory—, prays secretly and fervently for his fellow-man, weeping and lamenting. This is real love, the love which a monk is required to seek throughout his life. [6] St. Nilos the Anchorite saw monastic life as a spiritual altar upon which a Liturgy was perpetually offered up to God, which in turn was a source of blessing for the whole body of the Church.

THEOLOGIAN: I agree completely —replied the theologian. But then, why does the monk not engage in philanthropy along with his offering of prayer? Thus the love of God would be marvelously combined with a love for man. Why not staff the hospitals, hospices for the aged, etc. with monks and nuns, who are wholly detached from things of the world. In this way there would be no exploitation or tormenting of the sick and so on by various opportunists and self-seeking charlatans. Do you not agree?

MONK: I see, my son, that you are unable to relinquish the idea that the Christian, and in this case the monk, must couple his life, his spiritual course, with social action, philanthropic works, and the like. I would ask you: What did our *Panaghia*, the Mother of God —she who is more honorable than the Cherubim and incomparably more glorious than the Seraphim— do before the announcement of the Archangel Gabriel, who called her "Full of Grace"? It is not possible that she had any interaction with those around her, since she lived in the "Holy of Holies." And yet God rested fully within her. From her all-pure blood God fashioned, through the creative operation of the Holy Spirit, the flesh that was taken by Jesus, the Son and Word of God. And what did the Honorable Forerunner, St. John the Baptist, do, before he began his public preaching of repentance on the banks of the Jordan, that God should call him "greatest among them born of women"? Until he came forth to preach, he was, from the age of a young child, in the deserts of Jordan. Yet, according to tradition, he was counted worthy to be the forerunner of Christ both on earth and in Hades. And, moreover, even in his mother's womb he lept when the *Panaghia* went to meet St. Elizabeth —a forerunner, thus, even before his birth!

Chapter Three

"...Then say ye, We are unprofitable servants."

THEOLOGIAN: But perhaps, Elder —the young theologian interrupted—, the cases which you cite are exceptional and cannot be considered normal examples of spiritual life. In fact, we have Saints, such as Basil the Great and others, who literally exhausted themselves, both in body and soul, in their efforts to save their neighbor —and why not? We can cite even St. Anthony the Great. As I see it, in so far as you fail to give to your neighbor, you are also failing in attaining anything yourself. You see, it is this mentality which is in my blood, that is to say, that Christianity is incomprehensible without external charitable works.

MONK: However, my young friend, the instances of monastics active in the world are the exceptions to the rule, as you put it, for the lifelong sojourn of the monk is in the desert. Inasmuch as all of the efforts of the monastic are for the cleansing of the "inner man" from the "reprehensible passions," of necessity he must depart from the city, from men, and from the world. The world is like disturbed water. When you look into it, you cannot see your face. The desert, however, is like the calm water in a vessel, and in it you can see your face in detail. "The yearning for redemption mystically calls a man to the desert, towards silence, towards solitude."

It is for this reason that St. Basil the Great, before he went to the city (and he went, not on his own, but by Divine Will), went out into the desert and was purified in its crucible, being made a recipient of Grace, a chosen vessel. Thus he wrote: "For I abandoned my habitat in the city, the occasion for a myriad of evils." As for St. Anthony the Great, if you read his life, written by St. Athanasios the Great, you will see that this Teacher of the Desert went back to the world twice: one time to be martyred, burning as he was with divine love (would to God that we too might be so inflamed!); and the second time when, threatened by the heresy of Arius, the Church called him to strengthen the Faithful. It is worth noting that it was not necessary, in this second instance, for St. Anthony to speak and to philosophize; simply the sight of him was a source of benefit to the soul and a source of salvation. The following passage shows precisely what St. Anthony believed about a monastic's presence in the desert and in the world: "Again he [St. Anthony] said, 'Just as a fish tarrying long on the dry land will die, so monks delaying to return to their cell, or who spend their time with the worldly, are torn away from the disposition towards silence; as a fish to the sea, then, so must we hasten to our cells, lest in tarrying on the outside, we come to forget the protection from within.' " On another occasion, when the Saint was suffering from langour, he exclaimed: "Lord, I wish to be saved, but my thoughts impede me; what shall I do? ...How can I be saved?" And then he saw his Guardian Angel, who sat and worked, then stood, and then prayed. The Angel then said to him, "Do likewise and you will be saved." As you see , my brother, he did not say to St. Anthony, "Leave the desert and go into the cities to save the world." Rather, he told him to stay in the desert, to struggle there against himself and against his langour and against his passions.

30   The Monastic Life

THEOLOGIAN: Somehow —interrupted the young theologian—, I am beginning to see that you are right. But what prevents me from understanding fully your words? What prevents my escape from preoccupations with social action and works?

MONK: Listen, my child, the contemporary Christian in the world, entangled as he is in temporal concerns, has lost the essence of Christianity and, more specifically, of Orthodoxy —namely, mysticism, divine love. He believes that he has been appointed to the service of his neighbor and that, consequently, he does not have time for himself. He thinks that his giving of himself entirely to his neighbor is enough to show that he is not selfish or egotistical. However, the truly unselfish man is one who subjects himself to hardship through the ways of asceticism set forth and left to us by the Holy Fathers, not those hardships which contemporary zealots for "social action" desire, i.e., trips to hospitals, social agencies, etc. The truly unselfish man is likewise one who humbles himself, fleeing vainglory. Internally, he is humbled through self-denial and self-reproach, the beginning or *alpha* of mystical spiritual work. External humility lies in humble eyes cast downwards, in silence, in the avoidance of quarrels, in submission, in not contradicting one's superiors, in the avoidance of the provocation of others, in suffering insult, and in such things. Since, then, the "active Christian" betrays these mystical works of humility, he believes that he is able to cure others and has forgotten the words, "Physician, heal thyself" and the admonition, "My brethren, be not many masters, knowing that we shall receive the greater condemnation." The unfortunate "active Christian" has not reflected well: "How, indeed, will I give, when I do not have?" How will an empty cistern water the gardens? He has not reflected on what it is that a Christian *should have* and what he, himself, *has*. He has forgotten the words of St. Paul: "Nevertheless I live; yet not I, but Christ liveth in me," which words were the moving force of his apostolic activity.

So it is that the contemporary, supposedly "philanthropic" believer has abandoned the "spirit," devoting himself, rather, to the "letter," having adopted the mentality and teaching of the Latin Papacy: that good works should save him. All the same, the Lord says, "When ye shall have done all those things which are commanded you, say, We are unprofitable servants." Unfortunate is he who thinks that Heaven is bought with works....

THEOLOGIAN: Yes, but I thought that Christ said that He "will render unto every man according to his deeds..." —interjected the young theologian. How do you explain that?

MONK: Listen, my son. Christ is not speaking about works that merit Heaven or Hell, but about works done with faith in Him or without faith in Him. Christ will render unto each in proportion to the works he performed to avoid sin and to protect the purity he acquired at Baptism. For every good work, every virtue, helps us to avoid that which is opposed to it: purity of body aims to protect the body, or through it the soul, from defilement by debauchery or fornication; we pursue humility for the purpose of fleeing pride; meekness that we might avoid anger; care to counter negligence; prayer to hold off indifference; martyrdom to defy idolatry; and so on. [7] Thus, the avoidance of sin is a work of nature; that is, it is within the natural powers of man to avoid sin. One does not have to be a Christian to avoid what is sinful. But Christianity adds something to this abstinence from sin. The Grace of God —and mind this— adds sanctification to him who abstains from sin, and the initial purity of Baptism (which heretics and those who deny God lack) is maintained, thus making the person a holy receptacle in which God dwells. Both he who is outside of Grace and he who is within it may avoid sin, but one is yet wanting, while the other abounds in holiness, is filled with the gifts of the Holy Spirit, is cleansed in his soul, and is united, by Grace, to God.

THEOLOGIAN: Do you mean —the theologian broke in— that in doing a good work we should not be thinking that in this manner we are earning the Kingdom of Heaven?

MONK: Of course we should not. You should know that the Fathers divide the Faithful into three ranks: slaves, hirelings, and sons. The slaves do good for no other reason than they fear the punishment of the Lord if they do not keep His commandments. They are like those who also do good out of fear of being thrown into Hell. The hirelings, then, do good that they might receive reward, thus fulfilling the Lord's commandments for reason of recompense. They are like those who practice the virtues that God might grant them Paradise. These unfortunate ones, the hirelings, think that material gifts are able to buy them the immaterial and spiritual world, the Heavenly Kingdom, Eternity. [8]

There is, finally, the third rank of believers, in whom God fully rests. These are the sons of God. And who are the true sons of God? Very simple. Those who love Him and who do all that they do being moved by love for the Father: [9] that they not grieve Him, that they not appear thankless or ungrateful for all that He has given them —and all of this not to free themselves or out of fear or out of hope for reward, but out of a knowledge that they are saved by Grace alone, if the Father but pities them and shows compassion and mercy. Adoption — becoming a son of God and an heir of His Kingdom— is not a matter of good works, nor does God owe anything to us. Adoption is not a matter of obligation. It is given by Grace. [10]

THEOLOGIAN: I beg you, Elder, speak to me more extensively about the love of the believer, the "son," for God the Father and about the divine love (which, as you mentioned earlier, is the essence of Orthodoxy) that the contemporary believer has cast aside.

Chapter Four

"Divine love is madness...."

Father Isaac got up from his seat and moved away a few steps, lifting up his face and gazing toward the melancholic moon that had just risen over the peak of the mountain in front of them. The monotonous and distinctive sound of a cricket interrupted the touching silence. "Thou appointedst the darkness, and there was night." The moonlight was bright enough that the young theologian could see a few tears shining as they rolled down the the cheek of Elder Isaac. He was overcome, but did not speak. The moment was majestic, filled with mystical profundity. In a few moments, the chest of the holy monk began to tremble continuously from the heavy sobs which he could no longer contain. The monk had undergone a transformation. His lips uninterruptedly moved as he repeated the prayer of Jesus: "Lord Jesus Christ, Son of God, have mercy on me." After a bit, he sighed, "My Jesus, my Jesus...." The young theologian was at a loss. He had been an involuntary witness to these strange events. The city and its turmoil had never offered him such a sight.

* * *

THEOLOGIAN: Elder Isaac, what is it? —the theologian exclaimed, breaking the silence. What is happening to you? Tell me, what is it that I see and hear? Perhaps I am dreaming.

After some moments, the monk began to speak:

MONK: My beloved child, somewhere I read this, and I now offer it to you, for with experience I have seen its truth: "The love of Christ is the solution to the riddle of the desert, the answer to the enigma of the secret inclinations of our souls." So please, my son, love Christ. Then you will be able to understand what monasticism, mysticism, and Orthodoxy are and how much the contemporary world errs, having lost its way in externals and having exhausted itself in appearances, never hearing the evangelical voice: "Launch out into the deep." The soul of a monk, my son, like an abandoned bride, finds no peace.* Wounded by the sweetest divine love, it continually asks, "Have you seen Him Whom my soul loves?"

---

*Unfortunately, we find it necessary, here, to add a short note to the Western reader. In the West, owing to the ascendancy of secular thought, words which cast the spiritual life in the image of marriage are woefully misunderstood. Especially under the influence of Freudian thought, modern Western readers are apt to find sublimated sexual imagery in the beautiful literary device employed here. This tendency is reinforced by the fact that some medieval Latin mysticism, having deviated from the paradigm of ancient Christianity, certainly does, indeed, go beyond literary image by infusing into its aberrant spirituality unmistakable fleshly sensations. The reader must keep in mind that in the Orthodox spiritual world, which aims at a complete purification of the passions, marital imagery is restored to a lofty level. It is in the realm of the passions, in the Orthodox world-view, that one finds, in fact, a sublimation of the ultimate desire of the human being to acquire union with God. It is the world of passions which draws on the language of spirituality to exalt its fallen notion of love, desire, and union. Eroticism, a distorted and lowly force within the fallen man, is rightly restored in the spiritual man to the natural internal desire in each human being for union with and fulfillment in Christ. Likewise below, the imagery of aristocracy to describe the monastic state must be understood in the context of spiritual humility, which transforms the political associations that we might otherwise associate with it.

And it ceases not to ask this, exhausting itself until it finds its divine lover, the beloved Jesus. Oh and then! Rejoicing and jubilant, "shining, radiant, undergoing a most worthy and mysterious change," it enters into its mystical bridal-chamber with Him, through the inner veil, into the repository of the heart, there to behold the union of God with man in unutterable spiritual delight; there to be accomplished the inconceivable mystery, *theosis*, the saturation and permeation of the soul and body by the Grace of God. No longer does anything else interest the heart that loves Christ. That alone which the soul desires is the continual and unceasing delight and enjoyment of Jesus, the sweetest love. It delivers itself fully to the bridegroom, no longer belonging to itself. As St. Dionysios the Areopagite says: "Divine love is madness; it does not allow the beloved to belong any longer to themselves, but only to the lover."

Because of this, my child, I consider a life lived for the sake of external things both a crime and death for the soul. A man must turn within himself, so that his heart can be cleansed of its passions and so that Christ can come into spiritual union with it. God seeks a pure heart. He tells us: "Save yourself," not, "Save your brother." God is approached and He reveals His secrets through a loving heart, not through books or worldly wisdom. Christ first loved us and shed his Holy Blood for us. We also are obliged to suffer and to endure all for His love, just as he was not content to offer only His words. Monasticism is nothing else but a love for the bridegroom that increases daily and that floods the very being of the monastic. The monk knows that "remembrance of God is more salutary than breathing," as St. Gregory the Theologian says. The monk knows that every worldly attachment, be it the smallest, is spiritual adultery, for he should be completely fastened and devoted to his Beloved. Therefore, exhortations that he embrace "social activity" and pursue "philanthropy" in the midst of the tumult and distractions of the city are inconceivable within the sphere of a soul inflamed by divine love. Monasticism constitutes the aristocracy of the Church, and just as aristocrats spend their time in the courts of the rulers and take part in the "Lucullan feasts" and delights, so also monks always reside in monasteries, which are the antechambers of the Heavenly Blessedness, and there they drink the nectar of divine love. Intoxicated by its sweetness, they cry out: "We are wounded by love." [11]

* * *

Something strange had happened to Father Isaac. It was as though he were outside himself. He eyes were closed, his face completely tranquil. Only his lips moved. It was as though Christ were before him and he, with all of his heart, feared that the Lord might depart from him. His heart had been opened before the very eyes of the young theologian, revealing the secret experiences of a life spent in years of ascetic struggle.

Chapter Five

"No one has with ease ascended into Heaven."

THEOLOGIAN: How, Elder —yet again the theologian interrupted—, is someone in the world able to realize the things which you have told me —things that for me, at least, are difficult to comprehend—, when he is obliged to be concerned with the necessities of life, when he is troubled, and when he is beset by anxiety? The pace of life today is fast and materialistic. What can the believer do?

MONK: "The things that are impossible with men," my child, "are possible with God," and "where God so wills, the order of nature is overturned." Whatever else he may do, the believer who wishes to be saved, who wishes to be purified, must submit himself to deprivations and afflictions —in proportion, of course, to his psychological and bodily strength. [12] The whole of the Gospel and the Church Fathers literally shout and trumpet the message that salvation is interwoven with toil. To cast out demons, the Lord advises prayer and fasting. In another place, He exhorts the disciples to be vigilant and to pray, that they might not enter into temptation. Elsewhere, he cries: "How strait and narrow the way is which leadeth unto life, and few there be that find it." "We must through much tribulation enter into the kingdom of God." St. Paul, the great luminary and God-bearing Apostle, writes that he treated his body roughly, so that he would not appear as one unproved, practicing something contrary to that which he preached and causing scandal to others. In their lives, the Holy Apostles and Fathers show us, above all else, that asceticism is the mother of holiness. They also tell us that small afflictions and difficulties, undertaken for the love of God, are greater than great works undertaken without affliction. Naturally, none among those in the world is required to do that which is done by those in the desert. Yet a discerning and measured asceticism is necessary in the world, too, principally in the sense of one's detachment from inessential possessions and food. [13] It takes many hardships, pains, tears, and sighs for the Lord to open the door of His mercy. But why go on? Since the founder of our most holy Church lived an ascetic life, at the end taking up a heavy cross and enduring horrible bodily sufferings, it follows that the nature of His Church is also ascetical, as Her practice and tradition throughout the ages demonstrate.

...Time now passed. The melancholy moon had advanced well on its course. The cool of the evening had set in and the bodies of the two men sought warmer quarters. The wind, like the "Dew of Aermon," bent the branches of the trees, and the silent murmurings of nature created a wonderful mystagogy. The Elder continued:

MONK: Well, young man, as you can see, time has marched on. I must return to my duties and we must also rise early for the Services. Before we part, however, since you will be leaving early tomorrow, I would like to lay stress on those things which we discussed at the beginning of our conversation. Naturally, we have neither exhausted the subject of monasticism nor fully discussed it from all perspectives. However, there will be a future occasion when we can consider this subject more extensively.

Chapter Six

"To Govern with God!"

Let me repeat, then, and emphasize that monastics are not social parasites if they dwell in monasteries and occupy themselves with prayer and their own perfection. Monks and nuns, driven by divine love into monasteries and deserts, are like sparrows alone on a housetop, exiles wholly for the sake of God and inspired by Him. They struggle to be purified, to be released from the passions. In these places, they consume the devil and his passions with their prayer, making their hearts pure. In these places, they are illuminated by the Holy Spirit, being made holy and coming into union with God. There, they speak with God "as one speaks with his friends," being led by His Will. In all that God does, He readily takes into account the tears and sighs of His Saints, those who love Him. So it is that the holy monastic plays a part in the governance of the world. Do not let this statement alarm you or evoke disbelief. [14] Recall the Prophet Elias in the Old Testament who, by his prayers, closed the heavens for three and one half years. Recall the life of St. Paisios the Great, in which we learn that he delivered a monk from Hell by his prayers. It is in the life of St. Barsanouphios, however, that we find the clearest evidence that those who are holy, particularly monastics, govern together with God. He lived in a time when God was angered by an abundance of sin in the world. Disorder prevailed over all the earth. But there were three holy men at this time: John in Rome, Elias in Corinth, and Abba Barsanouphios in Jerusalem. These three calmed God's wrath, and so God did not pour out His anger on the sons of iniquity. Abba Barsanouphios had been closed off from these sinners for fifty years, having received the gift of binding and loosing the sins of Christians —despite the fact that he did not hold the Priestly rank— and of saving souls from hell by his prayers.

(Suddenly the young theologian interrupted the Elder with a deep sigh, saying:)

THEOLOGIAN: Where have those days gone? Nowadays, such monks have vanished. Today, instead of the laity finding models in such monks, they find harmful examples and keep away from monasteries, from the desert. There are no longer holy monks as there were then.

MONK: Forgive me, my young man, but you are not being fair. On the one hand you hasten to assert that there are no holy monks today, and yet you have not gone in search of them. Those who are holy do not, to be sure, go up on the rooftops and cry out, "Come to us! We are holy." They are hidden, rather, in the caves of the earth. And they do not put the treasure which they have obtained on display, for they fear the thievish demons and the vainglory that comes from praise. But as for the decline of monasticism, this has been facilitated by all of those who want Saints, and nothing but Saints, but who dedicate neither themselves nor their children to augmenting the ranks of the sound majority of monastics. And when they see a monk fall, instead of covering this exception with love, they trumpet it all over the community. They forget that all men, because of their weaknesses, fall and that the ideal of monasticism is not to blame. It is not so much the monastics themselves who are fired upon today, but the institution itself. And this is horrible, for this institution is founded by the Holy Spirit, God-given, and thus holy —for "every good gift and every perfect gift is from above, and cometh down from the Father of Lights."

I do not think that we can ever blame a contest because an athlete is unethical. It is always the athlete who is to blame. So, then, let those who reproach monasticism take heed in this matter, for they are heaping up great wrath upon their own heads.

If, my child, the world still exists, in spite of all of its corruption and ethical decay, it is because of the holy ascetics, monks, nuns, and hermits who, day and night and far away from Pharisaical displays, invisibly entreat the Most High —with groanings that cannot be uttered— to show patience and prolong His Mercy. According to St. John of the Ladder, prayer is a great, sweet, and beloved tyrant, standing before God and compelling Him to be merciful and show forbearance to the repentant soul. [15] You will remember, my brother, that in the Old Testament prayer caused the sun to stand still.

Do you see, then, what a Saint can offer? And you should know that after their deaths they offer us even more. Behold, young man, that however many the good works that a person in the world might offer for the benefit of man, they pale before the bounties we receive by the prayers of the holy desert dwellers.

The centrality of prayer, which I have spent so much time discussing, is not such that it compromises the importance of philanthropic works. I simply want to assure you that the endeavor to cleanse the heart and its works by prayer, along with asceticism founded in humility, is greater. Social action, properly speaking, should spring forth from a loving soul, not from some pietistic or sentimental love that is satisfied with external effusions and material gifts alone. Good works lie in holiness that has been externalized, and they have a purely instructive character, benefiting and accruing principally to the doer and not to the receiver. They are done, as it were, for the perfecting of the benevolent soul. As we have said, good works must, of course, be undertaken by the laymen, even before sanctification has been achieved, but without a lopsided emphasis on their significance.

Chapter Seven

"No amount of water can extinguish love."

In a few words, brother, you have seen how beneficial the holy monastic is and how improper and unreasonable it is, today, to want to take the holy prayer rope from his hands and give him pens, or scissors, or bandages to hold. How foolish it is to wish that the monastic be no longer fragrant from incense, but that he smell of ink or iodine. Imagine how untraditional are those things which our contemporaries desire: to take from the monastic the holy mourning and gladdening sorrow of the Cross and Resurrection, and to bestow on him a "pietistic" smile that will not reproach others for their sins or for their comfortable ways of life.

Indeed, my brother, it is the modern man, who has experienced nothing of the mystical Paradise of Orthodoxy given to us in monasticism by the Fathers, who wants a Christianity without love, a Christianity in which the "love of the desert" would be missing, free of the ascetic love of Jesus and the ascetic song of the betrothed soul for her beloved Jesus. Modern man desires that we betray the experience of ascetic love. He attempts to approach and understand God through books. He takes pride in the fact that he is called a theologian, even though only those who are pure in heart are actually theologians.

Father Isaac finished with these words and, upon rising, bid the young theologian farewell, quickly disappearing into the darkness as he walked toward his cell, where, with his ardent prayer, he would assail

Heaven until the morning hours.

> "Angels, a light to monks;
> And monks, a light to
> those in the world."

The Ladder

EPILOGUE

"In this is contained every working of the commandments. For there is nothing higher than the love of God."

From the conversation which we have just recounted, every believer can see that the institution of monasticism is not one to which all of the current outlandish calumnies and critcisms should be imputed.

The path set forth for us by the Fathers, "who took wings in the desert," continues today and will continue until the consummation of the ages. This is the path of "eminent love." It entails scorn for that which is earthly, engendered by this love, and the ceaseless recollection in the heart of the Beloved One, the "desert's love," the sweetest Jesus.

If one were to imagine the disappearance of men inflamed by divine love, then monasticism would automatically disappear. It would be no longer necessary for men to live in the deserts and caves of the earth, as nothing would in any way bind them to these places. Then, even without the enactment of programs or laws to remove them or the promulgation of encyclicals against them, the beloved desert would weep for her children, those who would otherwise love her. Choosing not the wonderful beauty of the desert, but the seduction and vainglory of the world, "the deceitfulness of this world," men will have become spiritual adulterers.

Let modern activist Christians, then, stop their senseless shouting about the need for monastics to go down into the cities and to engage in social action.

Let the modern "Fathers" apply themselves to the literature of the desert and abandon the cheap literature of the West, filled as it is with rationalism, the truly "frozen product" of the heterodox North that lacks the salt of the All-Holy Spirit.

Let these modernists allow the desert dwellers to pray for their salvation and for that of the world, far removed from the world.

Let these same leave the monks in silence in their caves and eagles' haunts, always there to love their delightful and ever-desired Jesus, Who first loved us and Who was sacrificed for our sins, Who fervently desires that we pursue the betrothal of our souls to Him all the days of our lives, and to Whom be glory and dominion, with His unoriginate Father and the Holy Spirit, unto the ages. Amen.

Notes

1. It is a great deception, and one trumpeted about much today, to believe that one will "save" the world and deliver it from its misfortunes. Works of love directed towards one's neighbors are performed mainly for the benefit and purification, by the Lord's Grace, of the doer. For the All-Good God can sustain and adorn all, just as He adorns and sustains the inanimate world. If He sustains the inanimate world, will He then abandon the poor, for whom He was crucified, to chance? Let us remember His holy words: "Behold the fowls of the air: for they sow not, neither do they reap, nor gather into barns; yet your heavenly Father feedeth them.... Consider the lilies of the field, how they grow; they toil not, neither do they spin: ...yet even Solomon in all his glory was not arrayed like one of these" (St. Matthew 16: 26-29).

2. "The sign of unfeigned love is the forgiveness of even unjust accusations. For so also the Lord loved the world." (St. Mark the Ascetic)

3. It is good to benefit inquirers with a word. But better yet to aid them with prayer and virtue. For if one offers himself to God on their account, along with him God helps the neighbor, too, with His own assistance." (St. Mark the Ascetic)

4. That is to say, the works of the desert, of asceticism based on humility: fasting, vigils, prayer.

5. Philanthropic works performed without hu-

mility and prayer not only fail to benefit the soul, but harm it. Those who perform such works with conceit and pride, as though they supposedly have done something important, are like the Pharisees and will hear those frightful words on the Day of Judgment: "I never knew you: depart from me, ye that work iniquity." And being at a loss, the modern-day Pharisees will say, "Lord, Lord, have we not prophesied in thy name? and in thy name cast out devils? and in thy name done many wonderful works?" But the Lord will say, "I wanted to dwell in your heart —for this is what causes me the greatest joy— and be united to you, but you did not take care to cleanse it of the passions. To the contrary, you soiled it even more with your filthy pride. I loved you intensely, running behind you all of the days of your life, hoping that you would give me an opportunity to enter into the chamber of your heart. But you scorned me. Depart from me, for I do not know you."

6. Here we shall say something that is perhaps bold: The monk who does not pray for the rest of mankind, especially those in the world, does not fulfill his responsibility. If the monk does not pray for his brother, who shall pray? We believe that the monk who does not feel the pain of others in his prayers has no favor before God. This, of course, holds for all of the Faithful, but it is in particular absolutely so for those living in the desert.

7. As this subject is important, we quote here a passage from St. Mark the Ascetic:

> 22) When Scripture says, "He will reward every man according to his works" (St. Matt. 16:27), do not imagine that works in themselves merit ei-

ther hell or the kingdom. On the contrary, Christ rewards each man according to whether his works are done with faith or without faith in Himself; and He is not a dealer bound by contract, but God our Creator and Redeemer.

23) We who have received baptism offer good works, not by way of repayment, but to preserve the purity given to us.

24) Every good work which we perform through our own natural powers causes us to refrain from the corresponding sin; but without grace it cannot contribute to our sanctification.

25) The self-controlled refrain from gluttony; those who have renounced possessions, from greed; the tranquil, from loquacity; the pure, from self-indulgence; the modest, from unchastity; the self-dependent, from avarice; the gentle, from agitation; the humble, from self-esteem; the obedient, from quarrelling; the self-critical, from hypocrisy. Similarly, those who pray are protected from despair; the poor, from having many possessions; confessors of the faith, from its denial; martyrs, from idolatry. Do you see how every virtue that is performed even to the point of death is nothing other than refraining from sin? Now to refrain from sin is a work within our own natural powers, but not something that buys us the kingdom.

St. Mark the Ascetic, "On Those who Think that They are Made Righteous by Works: Two Hundred and Twenty-Six Texts," in *The Philokalia*, vol. 1, trans. and ed. by G.E.H. Palmer *et al.* (London, 1979). P. 127.

8. "He who does good and seeks repayment does

not serve God, but his own will." (St. Mark the Ascetic)

9. Through abstention from sin, as we said previously, we preserve the purity of Baptism. Behold, then, love: in that God greatly desires to unite with us —that is, to come within our hearts— in our abstention from sin, we prepare the place where He will dwell. A true child is always concerned to give his father rest and to do that which pleases him.

10. "If, according to the Scriptures, Christ died for us (Rom. 5:8), and we live not unto ourselves, but unto Him Who died for us and rose again (II Cor. 5:15), it is evident that we are obliged to serve Him unto death. How, then, can we reckon adoption as something which is our due?" (St. Mark the Ascetic)

11. "Love ...in its activity is inebriation of the soul." (St. John of the Ladder)

12. "A seed does not grow without earth and water; and a man does not profit except by voluntary sufferings and divine help." "Being a lover of learning, also become a lover of suffering. For knowledge that is effete inflates a man." (St. Mark the Ascetic)

"Asceticism is the mother of sanctification, from which is born one's first taste of the understanding of Christ's Mysteries, which is also called the first level of knowledge of the Holy Spirit." (St. Isaac the Syrian)

13. "He who wishes to cross the spiritual sea practices patience, humility, vigilance, and temperance. If he wishes to embark on this crossing hastily,

without these four, he troubles his heart and is unable to cross." (St. Mark the Ascetic)

14. "Nothing is stronger in action than prayer; and nothing is more effective in winning God's mercy." (St. Mark the Ascetic)

15. "For prayer is a devout tyrant to God." (St. John of the Ladder)